PRAISE FOR "ADVOCACY MADE EASY"

"For more than seven years, Cynthia was a strong voice in my community speaking out in partnership with people living in poverty. Involved constituents like her are invaluable assets to our policymakers. With so many pressing demands in Washington and our state capitals, persistent voices like Cynthia's help drive positive change. I consider her a valuable voice and friend. Cynthia's methods of activism are the gold standard of citizen engagement and this book is a must-read for anyone looking to get more involved and improve their community!"

—Congresswoman Jan Schakowsky

"Levin shares clear instructions for impactful actions, so everyone can join in and make the world a better place."

—Shannon Watts
Founder, Moms Demand Action
Author, *Fight Like a Mother* and *Fired Up*

"Levin has created a powerful roadmap for change-agents. She shares how people can come together to create transformational change in the world. I have seen her put these lessons into action as an advocate for the global humanitarian organization CARE and I know, first-hand, that she perfectly embodies the values and the lessons of this terrific book."

—Michelle Nunn
President and CEO of CARE

"Since I first moved to Washington, D.C., thirty years ago, by far the most important thing I've learned is the power of passionate, committed advocates to effect change. Not paid lobbyists, not PR firms—but thoughtful, informed constituents who move their members of Congress into action. Any skeptic of that view should meet Cynthia Changyit Levin. Congressional staff and members of Congress know Cynthia by name and by reputation. And now she's sharing what she's learned to help others experience their power to shape political decisions—at a time when this has never been more important."

—Dr. Joanne Carter
Executive Director of RESULTS

"Advocacy is one of the most powerful tools for citizens to use our voices to influence policies and create lasting change that improves lives! Cynthia Changyit Levin has been a powerful advocate for ONE. Her voice has helped create meaningful change as we fight for the investments needed to promote economic opportunities and healthier lives. In *Advocacy Made Easy*, she teaches others how to most effectively engage in meaningful advocacy actions to make sure members of Congress hear from those they represent."

—Ndidi Okonkwo Nwuneli
President and CEO of The ONE Campaign

"With so many Americans asking, 'What can I do?' Cynthia Changyit Levin's book *Advocacy Made Easy* couldn't have come at a better time. Read it and rejoice—and then get into action."

—Sam Daley-Harris
Founder, RESULTS and Civic Courage
Author, *Reclaiming Our Democracy*

"If we assume that the policy advocacy needed to eliminate poverty, arrest climate change, and accomplish other urgent and worthy goals must be done by experts who can devote their entire lives to this work, we're sunk as a country and as a civilization. Empowering citizens to roll up their sleeves, learn the issues, and speak up for crucial policy changes is our only hope. Demystifying activism has never been more important, and Levin gets the job done brilliantly."

—Alex Counts
Founder, Grameen Foundation
Adjunct Professor, Johns Hopkins University
Author, *Changing the World Without Losing Your Mind*
and *When in Doubt, Ask for More*

Advocacy
MADE
EASY

Advocacy
MADE
EASY

HOW TO TURN CIVIC FRUSTRATION INTO POWERFUL ACTION

CYNTHIA CHANGYIT LEVIN

PYP **Publish** Your Purpose

For permission requests, write to the publisher, addressed "Attention: Permissions Coordinator," at the address below.

Publish Your Purpose
141 Weston Street, #155

Hartford, CT, 06141

PYP **Publish**
Your Purpose

The opinions expressed by the Author are not necessarily those held by Publish Your Purpose.

Ordering Information: Quantity sales and special discounts are available on quantity purchases by corporations, associations, and others. For details, contact the author at cynthia@changyit.com.

Edited by: Gail Marlene Schwartz, Gina Sartirana, Lily Capstick, and Kelsey Spence
Cover design by: Nelly Murariu
Typeset by: Amit Dey

ISBN: 979-8-88797-205-3 (hardcover)
ISBN: 979-8-88797-206-0 (paperback)
ISBN: 979-8-88797-207-7 (ebook)

Library of Congress Control Number: 2025915019

First edition, October 2025.

Publish Your Purpose is a hybrid publisher of non-fiction books. Our mission is to elevate the voices often excluded from traditional publishing. We intentionally seek out authors and storytellers with diverse backgrounds, life experiences, and unique perspectives to publish books that will make an impact in the world. Do you have a book idea you would like us to consider publishing? Please visit PublishYourPurpose. com for more information.

ACKNOWLEDGMENTS

TO DAVID, FOR ASKING me the right questions, so I could find my voice again. To my grown and flown kids. I hope you can find time to be happy as well as strong. To the staff of advocacy organizations who stay in the good fight daily supporting volunteers to take the actions in this book, especially Crickett Nicovich, Jos Linn, Lisa Marchal, Meredith Dodson, Rebecca Maxie, Lindsay Cobb, Misty Uribe, Charlie Harris, Brian Sweeney, Nicole Schmidt, Zach Schmidt, and Kristin Witte.

TABLE OF CONTENTS

YOU ARE NOT POWERLESS

I KNOW IT CAN seem like we are powerless. I know you disagree with some, or all, of the people elected to run your city, your state, and your country. The situation is bleak. Real people suffer because of policies that keep families in poverty, withhold medical care from those in need, damage the environment, deny rights to vulnerable people, and more. It feels like there's never enough good news to make up for the bad.

It doesn't look like we have a choice in what's happening to us. Do we have to live this way? What's the alternative?

The alternative is speaking out to decision-makers, empowering ourselves, and working with movements to change the world. This is the good stuff rarely taught in high school government classes! As a volunteer advocate, I feel alive and full of purpose when I help an idea become a law or prevent a harmful bill from passing.

We have buckets full of reasons that we don't speak up. I know we're all short on time and it's just easier not to express opinions to strangers. I also know most of our hesitation comes from a fear of the unknown. I'm offering you a shortcut through the fear that can lock us into inaction. With the clear and friendly instructions in this handbook, you'll quickly learn the basics of seven important advocacy actions. You'll feel more confident and less worried when you try something new in your activism.

Advocating will take persistence and courage. We'll do it for ourselves, and we'll do it for the people we are trying to protect. You will achieve more than you thought you could. Most importantly, you'll be able to say, "I did my part. I didn't just give up."

Can I guarantee that if you take the actions outlined in this book, your elected officials will listen to you and change their minds? No. But there is a 100 percent chance you won't change anything if you only vent your frustrations with your friends behind closed doors. I guarantee you will feel better than you do as an anxious bystander, hoping someone else will save us.

Advocacy Made Easy is about making activism accessible, friendly, and doable for everyone. I'm asking you to put aside the fear that keeps you from moving forward into a more powerful state of living.

Wouldn't you like to trade old, familiar feelings of desperation and frustration for the satisfaction and knowledge that you stood up at a certain time in history when you were needed? And, by the way, that "time in history" is any time you're reading this book. Because this is the moment when you're on the earth. This is the only time you get to make the world better.

Step out of your comfort zone. Do what makes you nervous. Let's see what we can achieve together.

CHAPTER 1

GETTING STARTED

GOVERNMENT IS COMPLICATED, BUT letting your elected officials know your opinions should not be. Advocacy at its core is simply expressing yourself to inspire action from another person with the power to help. It involves showing up when it counts and saying what you care about. As advocates, we can influence policy decisions and help define a future we all have a stake in.

Advocacy Made Easy is a summary of skills I learned during my transformation from an uncertain stay-at-home mom who had never made a phone call to Congress to an activist visiting congressional offices multiple times a year.

This "how-to" handbook will help take the stress out of your advocacy actions. Even with some experience in activism, new steps can be intimidating for anyone. My hope is that having real-life examples and clear advice can remove barriers in your way to becoming a powerful advocate.

The seven actions included are roughly organized in the order of time it takes to accomplish each task. Notice that I didn't say the tasks are organized based on "ease" or "effort." What is easy for one person may be a big challenge for someone else.

- ↩ The online action
- ↩ The phone call
- ↩ The handwritten letter
- ↩ The letter to the editor
- ↩ The op-ed
- ↩ The town hall meeting
- ↩ The lobby meeting

Of course, this isn't a comprehensive list of everything an activist can do. I've focused on actions available to us in the United States that are especially suited to sharing opinions, information, and ideas. Each of them can be used in combination with the others to increase influence and access with decision-makers. These are my favorite actions because they create opportunities for me to bring kindness, compassion, and empathy into my activism. They help me be true to myself in a combative political environment.

I personally work mostly on global causes, so much of my advice focuses on interacting with U.S. senators and representatives to influence federal policies. However, the actions I describe can be used at the state, county, city, school board, and neighborhood levels. Learn the basics from this book and then boldly and creatively adapt these general principles to fit your own situation and personality.

Take the action that fits you in the moment. It's likely that not all of them will sync with your capability or resources right now. That's okay! Your abilities and appetite for advocacy will change over time, allowing you to stretch yourself when the time is right.

Start with something that seems challenging, but achievable to you, so you can break that political inertia. Once you're in motion, you'll tend to stay in motion. Do something that is impressive to only you—don't worry about anyone else—and you'll give yourself the confidence to move onto even bigger acts.

Finding Your Elected Officials

For any advocacy action, you'll need to know the names and contact information of officials you want to influence. How do you find the contact information for your elected officials?

1. **Go to a search website.** Visit www.usa.gov/elected-officials/ or type "Find my member of Congress" in your favorite search engine to find similar websites.
2. **Enter your address.** If you live in a zip code shared by more than one representative, you may have to use your ZIP+4 code to get the name of your representative. You can find that number from the U.S. Postal Service website www.usps.com.
3. **Visit their websites.** Once you have the names of your elected officials, seek out their individual websites to get contact information for their local offices, so you can call, write, and visit in person.

Building Your Advocacy Village

If you feel you can't take some actions because you lack certain skills or resources, look at it as an opportunity to do some "village building." Bring in friends or colleagues who excel in the areas where you are uncertain. An action that seems right up the alley of a friend when it's not your cup of tea is a golden opportunity to

invite that friend to collaborate with you. When you offer someone the chance to help, they are likely to become more invested in
your cause. They might even join your local advocacy group!

Examine your to-do list and determine if you know individuals or organizations with resources to help with specific tasks. The
answer might be a public library or a house of worship. If you have
a group of advocates around you, you can start pooling resources
and asking specific questions like:

- Who has a car to help get to meetings?
- Who has a video conference account to help with remote
  group meetings or online lobby meetings with staff in D.C.?
- Who has the skills to proofread letters to the editor?
- Who has a room where everyone can meet?

It might be uncomfortable to ask for help, but I find volunteers want to be useful and add value to the group. Simple requests
can start to form a powerful team around you.

CHAPTER 2

MESSAGING WITH THE EPIC FORMAT

"In times past, I thought it was better to stay silent because my opinion wouldn't matter. But sharing space with others who believe in the same work and seeing actual change motivates me."

LaShaun Martin
National Vice President, Mocha Moms, Inc.
Baltimore, MD

ONE REASON PEOPLE FEEL intimidated about speaking out is that they don't know what to say. Let's address this right away, so you can jump into action! It can take some practice to come up with the right words to share. Sometimes advocacy organizations will provide sample text for you to customize for yourself, but the most powerful messages will be crafted by you.

I use several methods to create short letters or talks, but for simplicity, my favorite is the "EPIC" format I learned from

RESULTS organizers. It was originally a sales tool brought to RESULTS by a volunteer to help everyone have a place to start writing, but it became a strong tradition still used by the organization today. I've given the EPIC format its own chapter because it can be used for every action in this book.

Using this format helps order my scattered thoughts into clear, concise, and effective communications. It's useful for many kinds of actions, from handwritten letters to elevator pitches you might say to members of Congress in actual elevators on Capitol Hill. The letters of EPIC stand for **E**ngage, **P**roblem, **I**nform, and **C**all to Action.

- **Engage.** Engage the attention of your audience. You could use a question, a personal experience, startling statement, or even a thank-you to your member of Congress for an action you appreciated. Describing a personal connection to an issue can be a powerful beginning.
- **Problem.** Briefly state the problem you want your audience to address. I often add statistics.
- **Inform.** Inform the audience of a solution or illustrate how the solution can help.
- **Call to action.** *Clearly* state what you want your audience to do. Your call to action will be most effective if you can frame it in the form of a "yes or no" question.

My favorite part of EPIC is the Inform section. Most people never move from complaining about the problem. Yet we can't rely on our decision-makers to come to the same conclusions we do when we only tell them about a problem. Sharing details about a solution will set your writing or meeting apart from complainers and boost your credibility.

Look for ways you might employ the EPIC format in the actions throughout this book. You can find examples of it in my own media writing on my website at www.AdvocacyMadeEasy.com. But you don't have to go out on the internet for a sample. You can flip back a few pages and see I even used it in the introduction to this book.

Easy Does It:
Advocacy Stories

The term "elevator pitch" suggests a quick request you could deliver in the short time between entering an elevator with someone and arriving at their floor. This metaphorical scenario happened to ONE Campaign activist Matt Staniz with a senator on Capitol Hill!

Matt is a pastor of St. Luke Lutheran Church in Devon, Pennsylvania, who has lobbied about global health issues for fifteen years. His surprise encounter with his senator happened in Washington, D.C., in 2011, a little over a year after joining the organization. As he and ONE Regional Organizing Manager Brian Sweeney prepared to enter the office of Senator Robert Casey to drop off information about global AIDS programs, the senator suddenly came out of an unmarked door heading straight toward them. They saw their chance to intercept and speak in the hallway, but Senator Casey was in a rush and couldn't stop to talk. He said, "I have to get to the Senate floor. Would you ride in the elevator with me?"

While Matt took a nervous pause, Brian jumped in with an introduction of ONE. Regaining composure, Matt thanked the senator for leadership on the Global Food Security Act and asked him to support funding for PEPFAR (the President's Emergency Plan for AIDS Relief) and the Global

Fund for AIDS, TB and Malaria. He found it was just the right amount of time to acknowledge something good already happening and pivot to a related request. Matt sensed genuine gratitude and allyship when they recognized the senator's nutrition work. They didn't receive an immediate agreement, but Matt felt they had a moment of connection and raised awareness in the chance encounter.

Not having words instantly at hand caused an anxious moment for Matt, who was grateful for Brian's support. "I discovered having some sort of prepared 'Why I am here' statement is a good idea. Just one or two sentences can set the tone for a conversation." These days, he always has the elevator pitch for the ONE Campaign top of mind because he has more experience now. Yet he allows his past self some grace when he looks back, saying, "If I stepped in the elevator today, that part would pop out without any thought or work. But you have to do it for the first time at some point. You don't get comfortable or good at something until you try it and fumble through it."

Left to Right: Brian Sweeney, Senator Robert Casey, and Matt Staniz. Photo credit: Matt Staniz.

CHAPTER 3

THE ONLINE ACTION

"I could be sitting and having a cup of coffee, and I can just quickly shoot an email to my congressman's office that says, 'Hey, thanks for supporting Shot@ Life. Let's keep supporting global vaccines.'"

Yolanda Gordon
Volunteer, Shot@Life Campaign
Fort Mill, SC

WHILE YOU WILL ALWAYS hear me singing the praises of reaching out personally to aides and members of Congress, I recognize such meetings aren't ideal for everyone. What is a busy person to do? Use online tools! Internet resources are designed to connect people to congressional offices with ease. They make a good entry point for beginning advocates.

These tools can be very useful when:

⋅ An issue moves quickly and many advocates need to be notified immediately

- ◄ A person is so strapped for time that this is the only action they can take
- ◄ An organization wants to build broad awareness about an issue
- ◄ An organization wants to build up a database of people concerned about the issue

Rochelle Shane from Bloomfield Township, Michigan, is a fan of online actions. She's a member of MomsRising, a national organization known for online tools that help folks act on a variety of issues affecting the lives of mothers. Rochelle believes these online platforms are very valuable because they can reach a high volume of people very quickly and capture their feedback to Congress right away. "It's very effective because of how accessible it is," she says. "Regardless of where someone is, even if they are out somewhere, they are checking their social media. They can see an action right away without waiting. It's more convenient, and that's what makes it so productive!"

Let's look at common ways to advocate online and explore their pros and cons.

One-Click Online Petitions

You've probably seen petitions on your friends' social media posts. Fill in your address, click one button, and you're done. So easy! Your name and address will be added to a list of thousands of other supporters and delivered to the office of a specific person, like the president or the secretary of state.

Congressional offices are aware that these online petitions can be influenced by people using multiple email addresses, so they are not as effective as actions with a more personal touch. Still, it's a quick way to submit your opinion and an excellent way for organizations to identify allies. Once you take an online action with a group, they will have your contact information so they can encourage you to take the next step by either donating or taking a bigger action.

Web-Generated Emails

The upside of using email to contact an office is that you can comfortably type away at your keyboard. You don't have to find paper, a pen, envelopes, or stamps. A customized, personal email is a good way to contact your member of Congress quickly. However, it can be a problem if you don't know what to write.

That's where web-generated email campaigns come in. These websites allow you to select from various talking points and type in your own personal touches to make the email message uniquely yours. When you press "send," it will instantly deliver messages to both of your senators and your representative all at the same time.

The trick here is that it is easy for offices to automatically sort out all the messages with the same wording as yours and send you an automatically generated response. Your opinion does get tallied with others, but it's kind of like robots talking to each other.

You might have more impact if you rewrite the sample email in your own words using the EPIC format, hit print, and then use the regular U.S. postal system to mail your message to the local district office of your member of Congress. That ensures an actual human will open your letter, read it, and forward it to another human who will respond to it. The more staff power an office must use to respond to your request, the more they notice it. But nothing beats the internet for speed!

Online "Letter to the Editor" Tools

This is by far my favorite kind of online advocacy aid. Letters to the editor published in local papers are great because they show your members of Congress that your community is publicly talking about your issue.

Your letter will potentially be seen by thousands of people via local media and will reach even more if it is posted or shared online. In addition, you can have friends and neighbors print out your letter and mail it to your member of Congress, saying they read your letter and agree with you.

Not as many activists write these letters because it can be daunting to come up with a succinct description of your issue in less than 200 words, which is the typical word limit for most letters to the editor. But many organizations offer online tools that provide a nice template you can customize, and some allow you to send it to your paper directly from the website. How cool is that?

Just be sure to rephrase your message in your own style—don't copy the template text word for word. A quick AI check can reveal identical letters published in other publications. If more than a few people submit a letter duplicated from a template, you run the risk of not being published or even being banned from the newspaper. Writing your own letter in the EPIC format and submitting through an online tool will side-step this problem nicely. One exception to the rule of avoiding exact copying from the template: copying the "call to action" line is acceptable because you want to ensure your request matches the request of your organization.

CHAPTER 4

THE PHONE CALL

"I call Congress about three times a week during the
day, always squeezing it in between other things, so
I can talk to a real human. It doesn't take much time
and it's the easiest thing in the world to do. When
I hang up, I feel great because I've had a moment of
having my voice heard."

Alix Gordon
Volunteer, CARE Action
Miami, FL

TONGUE-TIED. HEART POUNDING. I approached my
phone like it was some sort of direct line to the president.

I was making my first call to my member of Congress. I'm not
sure why I was so scared. I must have been afraid that someone on
the other end was going to challenge my ideas or berate me for
speaking up. Guess what? That never happened.

Calling Congress is not difficult or time-consuming, once you
get over being nervous. But your calls can have profound effects on

public policy. Let me break down the process of calling Congress so I can spare you the stress I once felt. You can even make the calls fun!

It's Super Easy

Even though I was a tad freaked out the first time I did it, these days I usually call Congress while I'm multitasking: doing laundry, making lunch, whatever. It does not have to take your full attention or much of your time to call. It's so easy that kids can do it too. My own children regularly called Congress from grade school age through to their high school years. Learning to do this quick act on a daily basis gave a positive boost to my eldest child Yara who shared the following in a speech to classmates in seventh grade: "If there's anything in it at all for me, it is that I feel empowered and connected after doing it. And personally, that's how I want to feel at the beginning of every day."

You Won't Be Talking to a Member of Congress

Relax! The person picking up the phone will almost certainly be a staffer who is not a specialist on your issue. The job of that person is to politely take your message, write it down, and get your name and your address or zip code to ensure you're a constituent.

The staffers keep a tally of opinions from callers. You might think your phone call will be too minor to matter, but if your topic is hot in the news, you won't be the only one calling. Your voice will join with allies you don't even know. Your opponents are likely calling in as well. Don't let them have the last word without you chiming in.

Help Is Available

Most advocacy organizations will supply talking points and information you can refer to during your call. In fact, most will provide a sample script that you can customize to make it personal. A website called "5 Calls," found at www.5calls.org, offers sample scripts for over fifty different issues. When you enter your street address and select an issue, the site provides a summary of information, phone numbers for all offices of your U.S. members of Congress, and a suggested call script.

Calling Can Be More Fun with Friends

Have a little call-in party. Each call only lasts two minutes, so you could fit in a few calls on a short coffee break with others. Heck, if there is a line at the coffee shop, your group might have ten calls completed by the time the barista hands you your latte.

I also host call-in parties on Zoom. It might sound a little strange, but it's fun for friends to check in from all over the country. I put the sample script for the call in the chat box or on a screen to share. People pop in, mute their sound while they make calls, then stick around for a little bit to chat.

☼ Tips and Ideas

Tip for a quick confidence boost

When everything else in my day is spinning out of control, I feel strengthened by making a phone call to Congress. I can hang up the phone after leaving my ten-second message and think, "There. I did that. I helped." Other things might still go wrong, but after I've made that call, no one can take that feeling away from me.

Sample Script

To make it even easier, I'll give you a sample of a bare-bones call-in script. This script relates to nutrition, but you can take the basic idea and modify it for your issue. You can add flowery language and details about the issue to extend it by another twenty or thirty seconds, but this script will get you started.

> **Aide**: Hello. Congressman Bell's office.
>
> **Me**: Hi, I'm Cynthia Changyit Levin, a constituent, with a message for the Congressman.
>
> **Aide**: Go ahead, please.
>
> **Me**: I'd like him to support H.R. 1464, the MODERN WIC Act. WIC is the Special Supplemental Nutrition Program for Women, Infants, and Children. It's a U.S. nutrition program for pregnant women, mothers, and children up to age five. This bipartisan bill proposes updates to WIC to improve the certification process for families to access benefits.
>
> **Aide**: Thank you, may I have your zip code?
>
> **Me**: 63104.
>
> **Aide**: Thank you. Have a good day.
>
> **Me**: Thank you. You, too.

Ta-da! Not so bad, is it?

You might notice this is not the whole EPIC format. You could write a more complete script, but phone calls are quick. They can just focus on the "Inform" and "Call to Action" sections of EPIC. The most important parts of the call are the bill number (if your issue has one) and your zip code to let the office know you are a constituent. Compose your own message or find a script from an advocacy organization you trust. Then, just pick up the phone and dial.

Easy Does It: Advocacy Stories

Making phone calls to elected officials makes Jennifer Burden of Holmdel, New Jersey, uncomfortable. Jennifer was a trained volunteer with the UN Foundation's Shot@Life campaign when she lobbied for global vaccine access. She enjoyed sharing her views in face-to-face meetings and wouldn't hesitate to sit down with a senator. However, a day came when a phone call was the fastest, most effective way to advocate for vaccines in the United States, and she found that task much harder for her than any office visit.

In the midst of U.S. measles outbreaks in 2015, New Jersey Governor Chris Christie declared that vaccine decisions should be left up to the judgment of parents instead of the government. Jennifer believes that vaccines should not be optional for measles. Because of her work with Every Child By Two—an organization advocating for vaccines for American children now known as Vaccinate Your Family—she felt well-informed and outraged at his remarks.

As Christie's constituent, she was one of the few people in the country who could even leave a message that his office would accept. Yet the phone call intimidated her, despite all of her in-person advocacy experiences. "I am very comfortable reading and responding to body language during an in-person discussion. It is like a superpower that I can't use in a phone conversation!"

Nevertheless, she knew the phone was the best way to get her message across in that moment, so she made the call to her governor's office. Her heart was racing, as an aide noted her comment. "I felt so empowered afterward. During the call, I was so nervous. I kept thinking, 'What if I get Chris Christie himself on the phone?'"

Jennifer knew in her head that the governor wouldn't personally answer his main office line, but her irrational fear still felt very real as she dialed the numbers.

Ultimately, she decided the uneasiness she would feel on the line with an office assistant would be far less important than the suffering of a child who needlessly contracted measles. She drew courage from thinking of children in our country who could not have vaccines for various medical reasons—newborns and kids with immunity issues—and who needed the protection of herd immunity.

Because she empathizes strongly with mothers of those children at risk, she accepted her own discomfort for their sake.

Jennifer Burden changed her Facebook profile picture to this confident image after making her first advocacy phone call.
Photo credit: Jennifer Burden.

Shortly after she made the call, she changed her Facebook profile image to a photo of herself standing at a podium. She wanted the whole world to see her as she saw herself: a strong woman not afraid to speak her mind. "I want to be that girl in the picture, so confident and secure!"

Now give it a try! Here's a form to get you started. Just fill in the blanks and you'll be ready to make your call. Remember, it's not cheating to read right from your paper.

Phone Call "Cheat Sheet"

Hello! My name is (*your name*) _____.

I'm a constituent living in (*your city*) _____
and I'd like to leave a message for (*Senator/Representative*)
_____.

I'm concerned about . . .
(Give a one-sentence description of your concern.)

I would like (*Senator/Representative*) _____ **to . . .**
(Give a clear, one-sentence description of the action you'd like
them to take, including any bill names or number designations if
there is a specific piece of legislation you want them to support or
oppose.)

Do you need my address or zip code?
(Provide if necessary)

Thank you for taking my comment. Have a nice day!
(*GREAT JOB! Now, do a little dance and treat yourself to a tasty
snack. You deserve it!*)

CHAPTER 5

THE HANDWRITTEN LETTER

"Four of us organizers helped our congregations write letters to Congress about nutrition. We went to visit our Congresswoman carrying multiple envelopes full of hundreds of handwritten letters. Each of us had a little talk prepared, but she interrupted, saying, 'I'm gonna stop you right there. I see you have stacks of letters. I've gotten others from you, and I came in today to tell you that I'm going to sign on because of your letters.' I felt proud of our people for using their voices. Those letters helped us unleash the power of community."

Reverend Dave Buerstetta
Volunteer, Bread for the World
Naperville, IL

WHEN I ENCOURAGE NEW advocates—young or old—to handwrite letters to Congress, they always ask, "Do we really have to write them by hand?" My answer is: yes!

I know that our digital age makes handwriting seem quaint, but unless you have a condition that makes it difficult for you to write, you should handwrite your letter to Congress for two reasons.

First, it sets your message apart from the masses of spam emails and social media posts hurled at Congress every hour. Handwriting letters is becoming a bit of a lost art. Like handwriting thank-you notes, hardly anyone ever does it anymore. So, when an office gets your handwritten letter, it will be more memorable.

Second, it shows you are authentic. Handwriting proves you didn't digitally copy someone else's message. Even if you duplicate a letter word for word by hand, you must take the time to look at each word and write it out with purposeful intention. The author of a handwritten letter did not blindly copy and paste something without even reading it.

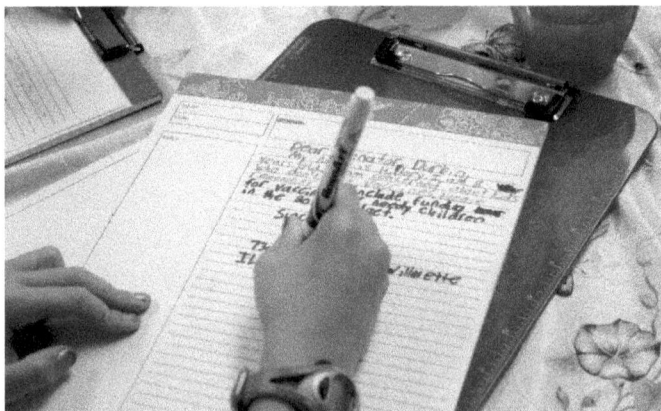

A young constituent used different-colored markers to make
her letter a work of art as well.

Writing Effective Letters

To write an effective letter to Congress, I recommend that you:

1. Keep it short and personal
2. Use the EPIC format
3. Present a clear request
4. Sign the letter with your name, title, and address
5. Don't overthink it

1. Keep It Short and Personal

The most effective letters share something personal about a constituent. Write about your experiences and why you care about the issue you want your member of Congress to address. Are you afraid you haven't personally experienced a story worth describing? That's okay. Describe a news story you heard or read and how it made you feel. That kind of anecdote even helps illustrate that your issue is important enough to be in the media. Your letter should not be longer than one page. Staying brief will help keep you focused and to the point.

2. Use the EPIC Format

I know it's hard to detail complicated human feelings in one page. The EPIC format can help you be concise whether you're starting a letter from scratch or working with a template you received from an advocacy organization.

Just one or two sentences in each section will do the trick. Here is an example of the body of an EPIC letter about low-income housing. The sections are labeled to illustrate the different categories.

Dear Senator,

(**Engage**) America is in a housing crisis. I recently helped a friend in poverty rent an apartment so her family could live in a safe community, and I learned how difficult this is for many Missourians.

(**Problem**) Millions of low-income working families struggle just to put a roof over their heads. Since 1960, renters' median earnings have gone up five percent while rents have risen by sixty-one percent.

(**Inform**) One way to address this problem is to shift tax resources to support a "Renters Tax Credit" for low- and moderate-income renters. This would give taxpayers a credit equal to any amount in rent that they pay over thirty percent of their income.

(**Call to Action**) Will you please support a renter's tax credit and prioritize low-income working families in the upcoming revisions to housing and tax policies?

3. Present a Clear Request

Make it crystal clear what action you want your member of Congress to take. It's best if you have a bill number and the official name of a bill, but even if you don't have that information, make your request for action so clear that you can put your request in the form of a "yes or no" question. It could be something like, "Will you help save the lives of moms and kids around the world by signing the Reach Every Mother and Child Act?" I underline or use a bright highlighter on my request sentence, so the reader can't possibly miss it.

4. Don't Forget to Sign

If you have an illegible signature like I do, it's important to print your name along with your address. Your address lets the office know that you live in their district and it's their job to represent you. Write your address both on the return address area of your outside envelope and on the inside letter itself. Busy office staffers move quickly, and your envelope may get separated from your letter. At best, you might not receive a response to your request. At worst, your letter might be thrown away if another staffer sees no proof that you're a constituent and a potential voter.

Using a title is optional, but feel free to use one. It can signal to your member that you have a place in your community and that you probably influence others who vote in their district. Titles aren't as hard to come by as you might think, even if you don't have a professional position. Do you sit on any volunteer committees? Are you a member of a religious community? Are you a Scout leader or a youth sports coach?

Even if you are just using talking points about global poverty from the CAREaction.org website, you're doing unpaid work for them, and that makes you an official CARE Action volunteer. Flaunt that title, baby.

5. Don't Overthink It

A letter to Congress shouldn't take you much more than five minutes to write. I've coached new folks who agonized over a letter for over thirty minutes, eventually taking it home for more tweaking. I wonder if they ever sent the letter at all.

Here's the truth: perfection isn't necessary. A hastily written message with poor handwriting is more effective than a masterpiece that never gets mailed.

☼ Tips and Ideas

Tips to get your letter delivered faster

Letters mailed to your local district offices arrive much faster than the ones mailed to Washington, D.C. If you mail your letter all the way to Capitol Hill, it will take more travel time, plus it will be held for another couple of weeks to get through anthrax bacteria screening.

Younger readers may not recall the anthrax bioterrorism attacks of 2001, which involved media outlets, U.S. Senate offices, and the State Department. Sadly, five people died and many people—including thirty-one Capitol Hill staffers—tested positive for anthrax.

Despite these attacks, local offices still receive mail without screening. Local aides log your opinion and then forward your letter to their D.C. office. I once had a Congresswoman who carried her own constituent letters back to D.C. every week in her own briefcase!

Write Often and Ask Others to Join You

Ideally, letter writing is combined with other forms of advocacy, and frequent letters will bolster the case of anyone arriving in a congressional office to speak about an issue in person. Even so, it usually takes many letters to inspire a member of Congress to take action.

Enlist neighbors, spouses, children, book clubs, and anyone you know to write letters with you. As a Bread for the World organizer for my church, I've collected and delivered hundreds of letters at a time from my congregation. That kind of citizen advocacy makes senators and representatives sit up and take notice.

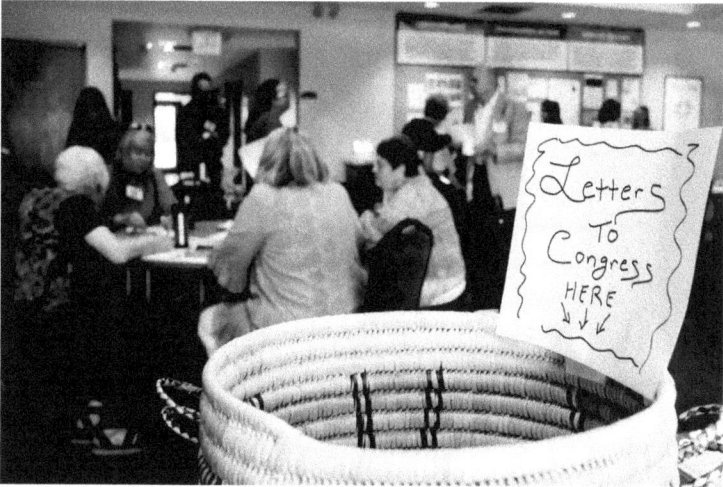

Congregants at Parkway United Church of Christ in St. Louis gather every year to write letters to Congress with Bread for the World about nutrition programs. Photo credit: David Levin.

What happens after they receive your letter? Most of the time you'll get a form letter in response. But don't let a form letter discourage you. Even if they oppose your view, a reply means a human took the time to read your handwritten letter enough to ascertain your position and sort it out for a response. If aides are doing that for hundreds of letters like yours, that's a good amount of time and energy spent on your cause. When you cause office resources to be used, you direct attention toward your issue.

You never know how far up the office chain your letter will go. In a lobby meeting I attended with students from John Burroughs School, Missouri State Senator Tracy McCreery asked high school students to send her more writing to read aloud on the floor during session. U.S. Senator Cory Booker read letters from constituents during his famous 2025 address that lasted twenty-five hours and five minutes. Those New Jersey letter-writers are now immortalized in a record-breaking historical speech!

CHAPTER 6

THE LETTER TO THE EDITOR

"I was fascinated that they [members of Congress]
wanted to hear my opinions, out-of-the-box ideas,
and different perspectives. I got hooked! I wanted
to learn everything I could to be a better advocate. I
started writing to my legislators, visiting their offices,
and writing letters to the editor."

Felisa Hilbert
Volunteer, Shot@Life Campaign
Broken Arrow, OK

A LETTER TO THE editor is a very short letter written by a reader and printed in the opinion section of a newspaper. It certainly takes a bit more work to be published in a professional newspaper than to post an opinion on your personal social media platform. Why make the time and effort to write one?

1. **To inform others in your community about your issue.**
   Your local newspaper gets delivered directly to more people than most can reach by hosting informational events.

2. **To attract the attention of members of Congress.** Congressional staff check the media every day to see what constituents in the community are saying about their bosses as a way for them to see what potential voters are talking about.

3. **To engage other activists.** Others can share it on social media, print it out, and mail it to members of Congress. They can even write their own supportive letters to the editor in response to yours.

Using methods I learned from RESULTS, I found that writing a letter to the editor isn't very different from writing a personal letter to Congress. But you must follow rules determined by the newspaper, which can generally be found in the opinion sections of a newspaper's print edition and website.

Small papers may publish every letter that meets their standards; larger papers publish only a fraction of the letters they receive. Follow the strategies below to boost your chances of getting published and to make your letters more effective.

Grab Attention in the First Line

People have pretty short attention spans, so your first line should be highly engaging. Can you think of an interesting angle that hooks the reader in to read more? Connecting to a recent national or local event always helps.

One of the easiest hooks to use is a reference to an article the newspaper has published previously. For instance, when a newspaper reported that a traveling college student was diagnosed on a Missouri campus with tuberculosis (TB), I used that local angle to talk about TB as a global problem that needs American financial support.

You will increase your odds of being chosen if you write a response to an article or someone else's letter to the editor published within the last seven days. Include the name of the piece and the date it was published in the first line of your letter. If you submit via email, make it obvious in your subject line that your letter is in reaction to a major event or in response to an article the newspaper printed. For example, your subject line could be: "Response to 'America Should Act Now to End Global Disease' printed 4/1."

Use the EPIC Format

You can construct your letter using the entire "EPIC" format. Remember to Engage the listener, state the Problem, Inform about a solution, and give a Call to action. As with the handwritten letter to Congress, all you really need is one line for each section. Of course, you don't have to adhere strictly to this format, but it can help you get started.

Be Concise and Precise

Most papers prefer to print letters between 150 and 200 words. Some will enforce a word limit very strictly and will not consider letters over a certain word count. The phrase "less is more" definitely applies here. An editor of my local newspaper, the *St. Louis Post-Dispatch*, shared that limits of physical space on the opinion page mean that editors prefer short, focused letters. Stick to one subject and stay on topic without rambling.

Correct grammar will also help your chances of being published. Have a friend proofread it if you can. Reading it out loud to myself helps me catch missing words that might unintentionally change the meaning of the whole piece.

Connect to Your Community

Help your readers understand why your issue matters to your community. That is ultimately what your members of Congress want to know. What experiences do readers have in common with people you seek to help? You could use the angle of summer vacation to explain how nutrition programs are necessary when many kids go hungry without school lunch. Sadly, most states have no shortage of articles about gun violence to relate to public safety.

Challenge Without Attack

It's healthy and engaging to question or criticize elected officials. Challenging the status quo is what an activist does. However, I recommend avoiding personal attacks. As tempting as they might be, they don't demonstrate the respect you want to receive yourself. Plus, they are rarely persuasive to people you want to win over to your position. Blatant insults might get cheers from your base, but they can firm up the resolve of your opponents and turn off those who are undecided about your position.

Also, if you are writing as a volunteer representing a nonpartisan organization, be careful not to damage its reputation by making remarks that maliciously criticize a particular political party, candidate, or civic leader.

Call Others to Action

End your letter by asking for specific action from your members of Congress. Mentioning their names increases the likelihood that they will see your letter because congressional offices conduct daily internet searches by the members' names. Make a clear request that leaves no room to doubt what action you want them to take. If you have a number for a bill or resolution, like "House Resolution 189," be sure to include it. Show them your passion for the issue and ask them to make a difference. You can also invite readers into action by asking them to call or write their elected officials.

Pay Attention to the Details

Include your name, address, email, and a phone number with your submission to the paper. The newspaper won't publish this personal information, but they might use it to contact you and confirm that you are the author. And be sure to check the Letters to the Editor page of your newspaper or its website for guidelines on submitting a letter. Some prefer emails; others require you to upload your words through an online form; others accept physical, mailed copies. Follow all instructions closely to give your letter the best chance for publication.

Write with Others

If you are coordinating with an advocacy group, send in several unique letters to the editor from different volunteers. Each person will bring their own distinctive writing style to the exercise. Having a choice of letters allows the editor to pick one that best fits the readership.

Whether the paper prints your letters or not, a group effort demonstrates that more than one person in the community is interested in a particular cause. This could influence editors to run more articles and opinion pieces about that issue.

"Write Letters, Send Them In"

Hands down, this is my favorite piece of advice from my media hero, RESULTS volunteer Willie Dickerson, who estimates he's been published over 1,000 times. He gets more media printed than any volunteer I've ever heard about, and he should! He has written at least one letter every single day for years.

When he says, "Write letters, send them in," he points out that a draft languishing on your computer won't be seen by an editor. Further, he's fond of reminding writers that 100 percent of the letters we never submit will never get published. Don't agonize over it so long that your hook becomes stale or you lose courage.

Even as an experienced letter-writer, I usually must submit five or ten letters to different newspapers to get one published. So, just keep writing and send 'em in!

EASY **Easy Does It:**
Advocacy Stories

My local RESULTS group in St. Louis generates about thirty published letters to the editor on poverty issues every year. Whenever one gets in a newspaper, group members hand-write notes on copies before we mail them to local congressional offices. So, each office receives piles of mail from us to be opened and responded to by junior aides. We met one of them in Senator Josh Hawley's office when we delivered a stack of constituent notes from a letter-writing event.

Months after that meeting, I attempted to schedule a Zoom meeting with an aide in Washington, D.C., who we had met with regularly. Unfortunately, that person no longer worked at the office. I was disappointed because new aides are often unfamiliar with issues and need to learn from the very beginning.

But when the replacement aide came onto the screen we cheered in recognition because there was our local staffer! He had accepted a promotion to work in the senator's Capitol Hill office. He was well acquainted with our names and the programs we wanted to talk about because he had personally opened and read our letters to the editor back in Missouri. It's very satisfying to think that we were training him for his new job.

Rest assured; real people read your letters.

Tips and Ideas

Tips to find your published letters

Newspapers will not always tell you when they run your letter. Keep track of where you submit. Then, visit their webpage occasionally to search for your name and some unique keywords from your writing. I've had some of my letters run unexpectedly over a month later!

CHAPTER 7

THE OP-ED

"Writing an op-ed is worth the extra effort because it gives you a better chance to personalize the issue. The first time you see your opinion published is a satisfying rush, like your voice is heard. And one voice can change everything."

Jeff Seale
Volunteer, ONE Campaign
St. Louis, MO

AN OP-ED IS AN OPINION piece between 500 and 700 words that is not written by the newspaper's editorial staff. Traditionally, these essays were physically printed in a position opposite the editorial page, so that you could see both pieces as you unfolded the newspaper. **Op**posite the **Ed**itorial, get it? That name doesn't really translate in a digital world, does it?

Op-eds are often written by industry experts, members of Congress, or other prominent individuals. But anyone can submit an op-ed! If an editor considers a piece well-written and of interest to subscribers, they may accept op-eds from an average reader.

Publishing an op-ed is a good way to control the narrative of your issue and build empathy for your cause. This kind of writing takes more effort. But when you get one published, it's worth it! I had eleven op-eds published in almost twenty years as an activist. Not too shabby, but small compared to the 120 or more letters to the editor of mine published in the same timeframe. Why?

First, op-eds take more time and care to write. The greater length means you need more creativity and writing skill to hold a reader's interest all the way to the end. I also take more time to research statistics and fact-check my wording since op-eds come under more scrutiny than letters to the editor. I spend about twenty minutes to write a letter to the editor and a few hours on a blog post, but sometimes several days to generate an op-ed.

Second, newspapers don't have as much room for them. They might post several letters to the editor with every edition yet only publish an op-ed from a reader once in a while.

Here are my best tips to boost your chances of an op-ed being published . . .

Grab Attention with a Compelling Hook

Use a creative idea, or "hook," in the first paragraph to engage an editor's interest. Simply referencing a past article isn't enough. Op-ed hooks tend to be clever, poignant, or very current. It doesn't need to be an inflammatory hot take, but it helps to have a twist on common thinking.

Here are some hooks I've used in published op-eds:

- Congress ending the child tax credit is like children behaving badly when moms aren't paying attention

- Contemplating the Saturn rocket replica at Space Camp and thinking the end of AIDS could be the next big "moonshot"
- Asking what elected officials did over summer vacation to protect kids from school shootings

Be Logical

You should take a reader on a deliberate journey from one thought to the next. If an editor sees your writing as rambling, your piece won't get past their desk.

When I struggle to get jumbled thoughts in order, I rely on the EPIC format to build a case for an action and engage the reader. In this case, however, each part might be a paragraph long instead of the one or two sentences you would use in a letter. There's even room to address a couple different aspects of an issue. Your format might look like, "Engage – Problem – Inform about a solution – another part of the Problem – more Information about the solution – Call to Action."

Be Personal and Original

With the longer word count of an op-ed, you can take the space to develop your personal connection to your issue. Editors want to publish unique and original work. A reader should be able to see why you're the right person to write the op-ed. It could be because of your lived experience with the issue or your perspective from a role you hold in the community (teacher, mother, doctor, food bank volunteer, etc.).

It's critical that your op-ed is original. Never copy and paste writing from another author and submit it as your own. This happened to me when a well-meaning fellow advocate mistook my writing for a template from an advocacy group. As a professional writer, it was crushing to see my words published under someone else's name. A copied op-ed might slip through and get published, but the worst outcome is that the copier or the original author could be flagged by a newspaper for plagiarism and banned from future publication.

Even if you use a sample template provided by an organization, don't submit it word for word. Add your own turns of phrases and personal details. These are the spicy elements that make opinion pieces so interesting to read.

Cautions About Artificial Intelligence

It's common for papers to care about exclusivity so much that they'll ask if you already submitted an op-ed for print elsewhere and decline your piece if it's not exclusive to them. Simply asking the question may be sufficient for some media outlets, but prominent publications have begun using artificial intelligence (AI) searches to check if words you submit have been published anywhere else.

Exercise caution using an AI writer to help generate your piece. It can quickly assemble an op-ed based on what other people have said out on the internet, but it can't capture your own personal experiences in life. AI-generated pieces look rather bland compared to the words of a passionate individual. Also, an AI writer is only as good as the information it learns from. If it learns from online misinformation or disinformation, you'll bear responsibility for spreading falsehoods in the media.

If you absolutely insist on using AI as a place to start a draft, take the effort to fact-check it and put yourself in the piece. Add personal touches to make it more appealing. Change phrasing to reflect your personal style. My college kid who works on a campus helping students with writing assignments tells me writing lab tutors can spot an AI piece a mile away because "it's usually laughably bad." Do not put yourself in the position of being judged poorly by college students.

Don't Give Up If You're Rejected

What if you spend all that time and effort on creating a masterpiece and it gets rejected? If they respond to you and pass on it, just submit to another paper right away. If you don't hear from an editor in a few days, send them an email with the subject line "Wanted to make sure you saw this piece about ____."

If you still don't hear anything in a week or two, send them an email saying you're withdrawing your piece and will submit elsewhere. That way, you formally told them and can honestly tell the next paper you have a fresh opinion piece not printed anywhere else.

All is not lost for unpublished op-eds. I like to think that no writing ever truly goes to waste. You could consider sending it to your members of Congress anyway or using it as a blog post for an advocacy group. I originally started my personal blog as a place for my misfit letters to the editor and op-eds that never found a home. Years later, I turned the blog into my first book! Who knows what can happen to your writing?

Easy Does It:
Advocacy Stories

Jane Klopfenstein of Edwardsville, Illinois, knew she had important things to share when the U.S. began withdrawing foreign aid support in 2025. Through years of leading a Bread for the World advocacy group, she worked with members of Congress promoting global nutrition programs. Jane knew how devastating it would be for families in extreme poverty to suddenly lose American food aid without warning.

She often writes short letters to the editor, but this time she wanted to reach a wider audience with a more persuasive message. She sent her 639-word op-ed in defense of USAID to a Missouri newspaper with wide readership about thirty miles from her home.

When the editor hadn't responded a week later, she checked the paper to find disappointing news. She said, "I labored for days on an op-ed I hoped would be worthy of the *St. Louis Post-Dispatch*, and I submitted it last Tuesday. I noticed all week that there were no op-eds at all, not even in the Sunday paper!"

Assuming her piece was rejected, Jane submitted it to the *Chicago Sun-Times* instead. Yet she was still curious about the disappearance of all op-eds from the St. Louis paper. She sent a polite email to the *Post-Dispatch* editor asking if the op-ed page had been discontinued. She also mentioned she's been a reader of the paper for over eighty years, starting in her parent's home.

The editor responded immediately, explaining the newspaper's parent company had technical problems restricting their ability to run op-eds in print. He also admitted he had simply missed her first email. He offered to run it on their website with an assurance he'd try to print it when he could.

Jane was delighted and dutifully wrote to the *Sun-Times* to withdraw the op-ed from that paper. The Chicago editor appreciated her diligence since they require first-run op-eds, and requested she edit down to a shorter word count for resubmission as a letter to the editor. Her persistence opened more ways to get her message out than she had originally hoped!

Jane also collects letters to Congress from her church every year for Bread for the World. Photo credit: Jane Klopfenstein.

CHAPTER 8

THE TOWN HALL MEETING

"For five years, we reached out to our Congressman in every possible way. In all that time, he only took one action toward our policy requests. Something changed at a town hall meeting. I stepped up to the microphone and publicly asked for his support. From then on, we had his attention!"

Margaret Smith
Volunteer, RESULTS
Dallas, TX

A TOWN HALL MEETING is an event hosted by an elected official, a congressional aide, or a candidate that is typically held at a public space so attendees can ask questions. These meetings might go by different names, such as Kitchen Table Talk or Constituent Coffee, but you can generally describe any gathering that allows the public to be active participants as a town hall meeting. These meetings can be very useful, especially if you have difficulty scheduling a meeting with your elected official.

Advocating at town hall meetings is like a two-for-one deal because you make yourself visible not only to your member of Congress but also to your community. A well-timed, thoughtful question will allow you to enhance your public reputation and may attract media attention. Plus, your member of Congress will answer on the record in front of the public and possibly the media!

These meetings allow ordinary citizens to hold their elected officials publicly accountable for actions. Some can get very rowdy when constituents are upset. This is democracy at its rawest—although not necessarily finest—form.

Finding a Town Hall

Be on the lookout for any town halls scheduled near you. Some members of Congress will list upcoming town halls on official websites. Some will publicize them on a mailing list. Some federal members hold town halls weekly in Washington, D.C., if you are lucky enough to be able to travel there. Sadly, others don't hold any at all.

Subscribe to the member's email newsletter and follow them on social media. Even if you don't like your elected official, subscribe and follow anyway. These are usually the first places they're likely to post about a town hall meeting. It makes sense that they would want to increase the odds of people showing up who agree with them. It makes their job easier if they don't have to answer challenging questions.

Make the Most of a Town Hall

The format for asking questions can vary from meeting to meeting. Questioners might be instructed to line up at microphones, raise their hands, or write down questions to be drawn at random from a bucket. I attended one at a public library where fewer than twenty people showed up, so an aide asked each person to state their concern in two minutes or less and responded to each participant personally.

- ↵ **Talk to someone who has attended a town hall with that member of Congress before.** Find out what the format will be and learn about their experiences with your particular member of Congress. Or, ask an aide to predict how the meeting will go.

- ↵ **Invite friends/allies to help.** An ally is important if you need an interpreter to speak for you or just a tall person who can raise their hand up very high! If you have a friend willing to also ask a question, you may want to sit separately in a big audience and try a "bird-dogging" strategy: having different people ask a similar question in a different way if the speaker tries to evade the issue.

- ↵ **Show up early.** This will allow you to find a seat near the front and might even give you a chance to connect with your elected official in a relaxed manner. I once arrived early and found myself parking next to my Congresswoman. As we walked from our cars to the door, we got to chat one-on-one without other people clamoring for her attention.

☀ Tips and Ideas

Dress for Success

Wear a T-shirt with the logo of your organization and sit in the front row. Even if you're not chosen to ask a question, you might show up in newspaper pictures the next day. Your shirt will remind everyone of your issue even if you never say a word.

How to Ask a Question at a Town Hall

- ↩ **Write out brief remarks that end with a clear "yes or no" question.** There's nothing wrong with reading from a paper if you are nervous.

- ↩ **Raise your hand right away if that is the format for choosing questions.** Be "first, fast, and high" and keep it up there!

- ↩ **Be brief and civil.** No one wants to listen to a meandering question, and hurling insults can be damaging to your cause or organization.

- ↩ **Share something personal about yourself.** Briefly tell everyone why you personally care about your issue, so other people can see themselves in your place. For instance, "I am a mother of young children who cares deeply about their health. When I found out that 1.5 million children per year—one every twenty seconds—die in developing countries because of a lack of vaccines, I was horrified."

- ↩ **Focus on the story more than statistics.** People are more likely to remember a touching story rather than a bunch of numbers. For example, after I shared statistics about how many children die without vaccines, my RESULTS colleague, Bob McMullen, used his turn to tell a story about a woman who personally vaccinated thousands of children. He concluded, "She just needs our help to get the vaccines!" If reporters are present, they might ask you to repeat your story for their audiences.

- ↩ **Address the audience as much as you address the member of Congress.** If possible, make eye contact with some of the audience as well as your representative. You could find like-minded people who want to join your group.

- **Use your loud speaking voice.** You want everyone to clearly hear about your issue and the name of your organization. Speak the truth even if your voice shakes.

- **Bring a fact sheet.** You'll usually be allowed to hand the speaker a paper with some facts and your request. That makes it efficient for them to give to the appropriate office aide to simply say, "Follow up on this!" instead of trying to remember what you said.

CHAPTER 9

THE LOBBY MEETING

"Each meeting with Congress makes me feel really
empowered and confident. Like I can do this, but not
just this . . . I can do life."

Candace Ellis
Volunteer, RESULTS
Belleville, IL

A LOBBY MEETING IS an in-person meeting with a member of Congress or an aide. The name comes from the old days when people routinely loitered in the lobby of a building to try to get face time as members entered or exited. The term "lobbyist" now has a bad reputation because we see paid industry lobbyists exercising disproportionate influence over lawmakers. However, volunteer lobbyists who visit their elected officials to advocate for humanitarian causes are lobbyists, too!

Most new advocates have a very hard time imagining themselves in a lobby meeting. Although a few are eager to look a member of Congress in the eye, it's not unusual to be intimidated by the idea. Even so, when I take nervous first-timers along with me for a lobby meeting, they always tell me afterward that it was exciting, and they usually want to do it again.

Lobbying allows for the most personal connection and opportunities for relationship building. That's why congressional offices reported that it's the most effective form of advocacy of all.[1] This type of action is most likely to influence a member of Congress who has not made a firm decision on an issue, so lobbying is worth all the time and energy you put into it. Senators and representatives know it's both daunting and logistically difficult for ordinary folks to meet with them in person. They tend to give more weight to our in-person requests than they give to phone calls or letters.

No one can predict exactly what your aide or member of Congress will say, but the more prepared you are, the better you will be able to handle unexpected situations.

Easy Does It:
Advocacy Stories

The first time I facilitated a face-to-face meeting with my congresswoman was a bit of a surprise for me. I thought my meeting would be with an aide, so I was startled when the door opened, and out came U.S. Representative Jan Schakowsky herself. I was extremely flustered and blurted out: "Hey! There you are!"

Smooth, right? I was nervous, but I was also prepared. All my practice kicked in, and the rest of the meeting went well.

---

[1] Bradford Fitch, Kathy Goldschmidt, & Nicole Folk Cooper, "Citizen-Centric Advocacy: The Untapped Power of Constituent Engagement," Congressional Management Foundation, 2017, http://www.congressfoundation.org/storage/documents/CMF_Pubs/cmf-citizen-centric-advocacy.pdf.

When the congresswoman respectfully challenged us on one of our requests, I thought my worst nightmare was happening in real life. But later, I looked back and thought, "Huh, my nightmare scenario really wasn't that bad. I did it. I can do anything!"

Cynthia and Congresswoman Jan Schakowsky
at a RESULTS reception in 2010.

Before the Meeting

- ↤ **Pick your issue.** Don't talk about everything that keeps you up at night. Choose one main topic and perhaps a second related issue to address if time allows.

- ↤ **Decide on your request.** Would you like them to cosign a bill or introduce a new bill? Perhaps you need them to vote against an amendment. Be as specific as you can.

- ↩ **Research your member online.** Knowing about their history and voting record can provide insight into how they might react to your message. If they oppose your position, you'll want to know that if possible before you walk in the door.

- ↩ **In a group preparation meeting, delegate roles.** Before you ever walk into the office, choose a leader to facilitate, someone to describe the issue, and someone to make your request.

- ↩ **Practice!** Whether with a group or just by yourself in front of a mirror, practice saying the words out loud so you're not tripping over any statistics or tricky terminology. Practicing for a little bit can help you be more conversational in the moment.

How to Schedule a Meeting

Scheduling a meeting with a member of Congress or an aide is a process that takes time and persistence. If possible, submit your meeting request a month before you want to see them, so you have plenty of time to work through these steps. Responses will vary between offices, but it's not unusual to take a few weeks to set up a meeting with an aide. Meeting face-to-face with a member may take much longer to arrange.

1. **Submit** a meeting request by using the office's website form. If you don't hear back in a week, move to Step 2.

2. **Call** the office for your member of Congress and determine the name and email address of the "scheduler" for the location where you want to meet (D.C. or local district office). Ask to speak to the scheduler directly with your request. If they are not available, send them an email.

3. **Follow up** every couple of days with polite emails and phone calls to the scheduler if you haven't heard back.

4. **Accept** a meeting with an aide if the member can't make it. Aides can play varying roles of messengers, issue experts, and gatekeepers. If you're meeting with an aide who covers your issue, you might be talking to someone who knows more about it than the member and plays the role of advisor. It's always worth building up good relations with the aides in the office.

TRY TO SEND A MONTH BEFORE YOU NEED TO MEET

From: Cynthia Changyit Levin < myemail@email.com>
Subject: Meeting Request for RESULTS constituents
Date: May 5, 2021
To: Jane Doe <Jane.Doe@mail.house.gov>

POLITE REMINDER THAT THEY REPRESENT YOU

Dear Representative _____,

SAYS "I CARE ENOUGH TO DO THIS FOR FREE!"

As a constituent and a volunteer with RESULTS, I am requesting the opportunity for 3-4 of our group members to meet with you on a Monday or Wednesday in June. WHEN DO YOU WANT TO MEET?

WHAT DOES YOUR ORG DO?

RESULTS is an international advocacy organization dedicated to ending poverty in the United States and around the world. We have over 100 chapters around the U.S., including three in the St. Louis area.

WHY DO YOU WANT TO MEET?

We would like to express in person our appreciation for your public service and also discuss support for the Global Fund to Fight AIDS, TB and Malaria.

SET A FRIENDLY, COLLABORATIVE TONE

We are especially interested in hearing about your own views on U.S. foreign aid as it relates to fighting global poverty. We wish to find ways we can work together as well as ways we can serve as a resource and support to you.

Thank you for considering our request.

WHO ARE YOU?

Sincerely,
Cynthia Changyit Levin
(she/her) — PRONOUNS
RESULTS volunteer
555-555-5555
myemail@email.com

GIVE YOURSELF A TITLE EVEN IF IT'S SIMPLY "VOLUNTEER"

HOW CAN THEY CONTACT YOU?

A meeting request email should contain all important information.

Tips to improve your chances of getting a meeting

- Be persistent, but not belligerent.
- Offer as much flexibility as possible for times and location.
- Accept a meeting with an aide if the congressperson is not available.
- Work with a respected nonpartisan organization.

What Should I Wear?

Most advocacy actions can be done while wearing yoga pants at home, but you'll want to look your best and convey respect in your attire for an in-person meeting or on screen. What would you wear to a religious service at a church, synagogue, or mosque if you want your appearance to convey respect to people you have never met before?

Think of a lobby meeting as a bit more casual than a job interview but more formal than a coffee date with a friend. I don't suggest wearing a suit if you don't normally wear one because you should feel as comfortable and genuine as possible. If you have a logo T-shirt provided by an organization you represent, you can wear it to the meeting. I like to dress up an organizational T-shirt with a jacket or sweater, but that's my personal preference.

If you are going to Capitol Hill in Washington, D.C., all day, the most important advice I can share is to wear comfortable shoes. Even if it means wearing athletic shoes with business attire, it's far better than blisters on your feet at the end of the day.

What Should I Do in the Meeting?

You have two objectives: to present your case for your request clearly and to advance a relationship with the other person.

What, exactly, is the case you should present? I'm going to let you in on the big secret: To be a powerful activist, your main job is to put yourself forward and say, "I care!" You are the top expert in knowing the reasons you care about your issue. As a constituent, the most important information to share with a member of Congress about your request is why you personally want them to do it. No academic scholar could ever know you better than you!

Yes, educating yourself about your subject is important, and knowing key facts can help. Yet the emotion in your voice and body language will convey your passion more than the actual words you use. As the oft-quoted saying goes, people will remember how you made them feel long after they have forgotten what you said.

This may be surprising, but your main objective is not necessarily to get agreement to your request in a single meeting. For requests they are hearing for the first time and lengthy pieces of legislation, it's standard for them to investigate the exact wording with due diligence before they sign. That's part of being a responsible representative of the people, and you want that to happen! An aide often won't even have the authority to approve or deny your request in the moment. You'll need persistent follow-up to get to a "yes or no" decision.

Every meeting is a little bit different, but I like to use this general five-step format to keep everyone focused and on track.

1. Make Introductions

Who is in the meeting? Introduce yourself, anyone with you, and any organizations you represent. Greet any aides in the room since you will probably be doing follow-up calls with them. Be sure to say you are a constituent and a volunteer. The fact that you live in their district means they are supposed to represent you. Your volunteerism demonstrates your personal commitment.

2. Say Thank You

Express gratitude for something the member of Congress has done on your issue recently. If they haven't done anything for you yet, thank them for making time for the meeting and for their service to our government. Many people launch right into complaints, so politeness can set you apart from the crowd.

3. Tell a Story

Use the EPIC format to help you craft a short speech about your issue. Try to use a story describing something you have seen yourself, someone else's experience that you have permission to share, or an excerpt from a newspaper article. If you don't think you have a good story, sincerely describe why the issue personally means so much to you. This is the part of the meeting where you want to emotionally connect with the aide or member of Congress.

4. Make Your Request

It is very important to make a clear request prompting a "yes or no" answer. The answer will likely be, "We'll look into this." Even if you get a "yes," be sure to get the name of the appropriate aide for follow-up to be sure they take your action later.

5. Ask for a Photo

A picture is not only a fun keepsake of the meeting, but it also serves as an image to post on social media along with a reminder about your request. You can still ask for a picture if you are meeting remotely on screen.

Tips and Ideas

Tips to keep your meeting on track

Politicians like to talk. Sometimes they do it to dodge a question, but most of the time they talk because it's in their nature and they are frequently sought out for quotes. Activists get frustrated when their valuable time to present an issue is cut short by a member of Congress rambling on about a pet project. I've even had a representative pull out a laminated chart and start to lecture from it!

How can you bring the conversation back to your agenda without being rude? Try these polite pivot phrases when your congressperson is off topic:

- "I want to be respectful of your time, so I'll get to the heart of the issue before you have to go ..."
- "Along those same lines ..."
- "Building on that idea ..."
- "I see we're getting close to the end of our time together, so let me bring us to our main request ..."

After the Meeting

Write a thank-you email to the member of Congress and/or the aide you met. If commitments were made in the meeting, repeat your understanding of them and say how much you are looking forward to seeing those things happen. Give yourself extra points if you also write another handwritten note and mail it to the office. Call the appropriate aide about a week after the meeting. If you don't take this step, it can be like the meeting never happened at all. The aide may get busy and forget to make the phone call to put the boss's name on the bill until you call to remind them. Or the congressperson may hope you won't appear again, so any commitment made during your visit may be easily abandoned. Do not let them off that easily!

How Do I Measure Success?

It is absolutely thrilling to walk out of a meeting with your representative's promise to sign onto a bill! I've had immediate commitments, but often the "yes" comes after a string of hearing "maybe" or even "no." It can be a long process, so you don't actually have to get agreement to your request to have a successful meeting. Call it a success if you got to tell your congressperson or aides a few things about your issue that they didn't know before or if your relationship with them progresses in some way.

I'll repeat this because it's so important: your main job is to put yourself forward and say, "I care!" If you told the aide or member about yourself and the reasons you personally care about your request, you succeeded. You can follow up later over email with statistics and updates on the issue. Starting a working relationship with a member or an aide means that you will have future opportunities to share more. Ideally, this is just one meeting among many more to come.

Volunteers often think they've done a poor job if they don't know answers to some questions asked by an aide or a member. On the contrary, it's great if you prompt anyone in the room to ask tough questions. That means you have them engaged and thinking. "I don't know, but I can find out," is a perfectly acceptable answer, and it also gives you a legitimate reason to call back in a day or two. It's all part of relationship building.

If your member of Congress is strongly opposed to your position, they will probably deny your request, but your visit may plant enough thoughts to prevent them from being an active opponent. It can be a "win" just to get someone to back off and stop being a roadblock!

Make sure to listen as much as you talk, avoid name-calling and labeling, and find something that you have in common (parenting, having the same hometown, or even owning the same kind of pet). That way you will make a connection that you can build on the next time you meet.

Yolanda Gordon, a RESULTS volunteer in South Carolina, often meets in offices that don't agree with her requests about nutrition and housing assistance for low-income Americans. She said, "You have to go through that journey to get to that moment to say, 'You know what? There's no way for me to fail.' All I can do is go and tell my truth, tell them what we need, walk out, and just be confident in what I did in that moment. Then, just let that sit." I agree. Speak truth to power and you will be able to claim success.

CHAPTER 10

WHAT'S NEXT?

"Focus on creative ways to close the gap between where you are and where you want to be. If one of those ways isn't working, don't sweat it, just try a different approach. Also, have patience because lasting change takes time, so celebrate every small victory you get along the way."

Andrea Riley
Volunteer, United Nations Association
Lincoln, NE

WHEN YOU KNOW WHAT to do, advocacy actions are much easier than they first appear. The next challenge is persistence. Ease comes with familiarity. Keep at it until it's not scary or hard anymore. Can you make it a part of a daily or weekly routine? A constituent who keeps coming back is much harder for offices to ignore.

If you realize that one or more of these actions feels more natural to you, scale up your activity to include friends who might be stuck in political doldrums. You can help others feel great about their contributions and multiply your own impact at the same time. Power is best when shared in community.

Could you hold casual letter-writing events in coffee shops or libraries? Would some of the writers drop off those letters to offices with you in person? Ask your new allies for help thinking of ways to make your events meaningful or fun while you amplify each other's voices. Acting in community is how we grow movements and change policy! As the late Supreme Court Justice Ruth Bader Ginsburg advised, "Fight for the things that you care about. But do it in a way that will lead others to join you."

Ready for more?

My best piece of advice for keeping up momentum is to join a reputable advocacy organization. The grit and determination required for activism comes so much easier when you're exposed to new ideas and inspiration. Keeping your spirits up is just as important as learning skills. If you can, meet regularly with other volunteer advocates to support each other over any barriers. That way you can have accountability partners both for advocacy and self-care.

Look for organizations dedicated to empowering volunteers. These groups are as passionate about helping you develop your own individual voice as they are about advancing their causes. Within my online list called "Recommended Advocacy Organizations," I've made special note of groups placing volunteer empowerment at the heart of their structure and core values.

QR code for my webpage with recommended
advocacy organizations.

Visit my website at www.AdvocacyMadeEasy.com with resources for more kinds of advocacy actions, a sign-up for my monthly newsletter, and links to my social media to keep in touch. I invite you to learn more about my personal journey from my book *From Changing Diapers to Changing the World: Why Moms Make Great Advocates and How to Get Started.*

Last Thoughts

Justice for all people will not be achieved in our lifetimes. Yet it must be nurtured through the years, decades, and centuries. If you've made it to these last sentences in this book, I think you know that you bear some of the responsibility to keep the flame of justice alive. But remember, you are not alone.

As I said in the introduction, now is the right time to act because this is the moment when you're on the earth. It's the only time we get to make the world better. Isn't it lucky we're here at the same time?

Keep going. Keep advocating.

GLOSSARY

Act: a bill that has passed to become an official law.

Activist: a person who campaigns to bring about political or social change. This could include working on legislation or public policy change.

Advocate (noun): a person who publicly supports or recommends a particular cause or policy to bring about political or social change.

Advocacy: actions taken to influence government policy.

Bill: a proposed piece of legislation going through the process of becoming a law.

Constituent: a citizen who lives in the voting area represented by a member of Congress.

House of Representatives: a governing body in the legislative branch of the U.S. government consisting of members elected from districts in a state. The number of representatives is proportional to the population of the state. There are 435 U.S. representatives.

Lobby (verb): meeting face-to-face with a member of Congress or an aide who represents them. The name comes from the days when people would loiter in the lobby of a building trying to meet with government officials.

Lobbyist: a person who meets with members of Congress or their aides to try to persuade them to take a certain position on an issue.

Member of Congress: an official elected by U.S. citizens. This book generally refers to members of Congress serving in the U.S. Senate or U.S. House of Representatives. Each state also has state legislators.

Representative: an elected official serving in the U.S. House of Representatives to represent people living in their district. The number of representatives in a state is determined by the population of the state.

Resolution: an official statement voted on by Congress to reflect a position held by the House of Representatives, the Senate, or both.

Senate: a governing body in the legislative branch of the U.S. government. There are two senators elected from each state. There are 100 U.S. senators.

Senator: an elected official serving in the U.S. Senate. Each senator represents the people living in their entire state.

The B Corp Movement

Dear Reader,

Thank you for reading this book and joining the Publish Your Purpose community! You are joining a special group of people who aim to make the world a better place.

Certified

Corporation

What's Publish Your Purpose About?

Our mission is to elevate the voices often excluded from traditional publishing. We intentionally seek out authors and storytellers with diverse backgrounds, life experiences, and unique perspectives to publish books that will make an impact in the world.

Beyond our books, we are focused on tangible, action-based change. As a woman- and LGBTQ+-owned company, we are committed to reducing inequality, lowering levels of poverty, creating a healthier environment, building stronger communities, and creating high-quality jobs with dignity and purpose.

As a Certified B Corporation, we use business as a force for good. We join a community of mission-driven companies building a more equitable, inclusive, and sustainable global economy. B Corporations must meet high standards of transparency, social and environmental performance, and accountability as determined by the nonprofit B Lab. The certification process is rigorous and ongoing (with a recertification requirement every three years).

How Do We Do This?

We intentionally partner with socially and economically disadvantaged businesses that meet our sustainability goals. We embrace and encourage our authors and employee's differences in race, age, color, disability, ethnicity, family or marital status, gender identity or expression, language, national origin, physical and mental ability, political affiliation, religion, sexual orientation, socio-economic status, veteran status, and other characteristics that make them unique.

Community is at the heart of everything we do—from our writing and publishing programs to contributing to social enterprise nonprofits like reSET (www.resetco.org) and our work in founding B Local Connecticut.

We are endlessly grateful to our authors, readers, and local community for being the driving force behind the equitable and sustainable world we are building together.

To connect with us online or publish with us, visit us at www.publishyourpurpose.com.

Elevating Your Voice,

Jenn T Grace

Jenn T. Grace
Founder, Publish Your Purpose